I0202116

Servat Corporation
P. O. Box 25153
Los Angeles, CA 90025
www.rumibooks.com   sales@rumibooks.com

Dedicated to All the Wonderful People

Past and Present

Who Set Fire to My Field of Thoughts

RUMI   GHAZALIAT SHAMS TABRIZI

RUMI   GHAZALIAT SHAMS TABRIZI

RUMI   MASNAVI MAANAVI

HAFEZ   DIVAN

SAADI   GOLESTAN

FEREYDOON MOSHIRI

SOHRAB SEPEHRI

NIMA YOOSHIJ

JAVAD AZAR

Molana Jalal Eldin Mohammad Balkhi Rumi is undoubtedly the most famous Iranian poet across the globe. His full name is Jalal Eldin Mohammad, known in the West as Rumi. He was born in Balkh on September 30, 1207 C.E. to Iranian parents.

Rumi's father, Baha Eldin Valad, was a brilliant scholar who taught in the city of Balkh, then part of the province of Khorasan, Iran. Baha Eldin was interested in the mystical aspects of Islam and was well versed in the Sufi concepts, which undoubtedly influenced Rumi's mystical view of life.

Baha Eldin moved his family from Balkh to the city of Konya, in Asia Minor, when Rumi was a teenager, presumably to avoid the increasingly destructive westward excursions by Genghis Khan (circa 1167-1227) and other Mongol rulers. At the time, Konya was at the crossroads of the three ancient cultures of Iran, Greece and Rome.

Rumi was 24 when his father died. After a seven year sabbatical abroad, he returned to Konya and started teaching when he was in his mid thirties, following in his father's footsteps.

Rumi's famous first encounter with Shams Tabrizi occurred during a 16 month period when Shams was in Konya. Shams Eldin Mohammad Ben Ali Ben Malekdad was born in Tabriz, Iran c.1186 and died c.1247. By historic accounts, he entered Konya on November 30, 1244 and left for Damascus on March 11, 1246.

Shams was forced to leave Konya for Damascus under pressure from Rumi's family members and followers who were fearful of his life changing influence on Rumi.

Rumi was unaware of Shams' departure for a month and when he realized that he had left for Damscus, he contacted Shams in writing and through emissaries, trying to persuade him to return to Konya.

Rumi's separation from Shams had such a devastating effect on his mental and physical health that Rumi's family and followers reconsidered and decided to bring Shams back to Konya.

Rumi's son, Sultan Valad, went to Damascus and eventually persuaded Shams to return to Konya after a 15 month hiatus.

However, Shams' second stay was quite short and he was forced by the same people to leave Konya in 1247, never to return.

Shams' second departure devastated Rumi. From 1247 to 1249 Rumi made two trips to Damascus in the hope of finding Shams, which were unsuccessful.

After losing hope of ever seeing Shams again, Rumi turned his poetic attention to Salah Eldin Zarkoob, whom he met in 1249. Rumi had a close relation with him until Salah Eldin's death on December 29, 1258. There are approximately fifty poems in Divan Shams that mention Salah Eldin's name.

After Salah Eldin's death, Rumi chose Hesam Eldin Chalabi as his muse and his successor. There are approximately twenty poems in Divan Shams that mention Hesam Eldin's name.

Rumi died in Konya on December 17, 1273. Poem number 14 in this book is believed to be his last poem.

My primary reason for translating selected Rumi poems from Farsi to English is to make his mystical poetry more accessible by using contemporary English words, symbols, and imagery.

The best English translations of Rumi's poetry are by Reynold A. Nicholson (1886-1945), who was a prominent scholar of Islamic literature and mysticism, and one of the greatest Rumi scholars and translators.

In my view, Nicholson's translations are hard to understand, and lack the amazing beauty of form and musicality that a Farsi speaking fan of Rumi sees and feels when he or she reads or hears Rumi's poetry in its original language.

I have tried to find the closest contemporary English words for the Farsi or Arabic ones used by Rumi, while trying not to lose their mystical concepts in translation.

I have also included English translations of poems by two other Iranian classical poets, Hafez (c. 1320-1390) and Saadi (c.1203-1294), as well as translations of contemporary poems by Fereydoon Moshiri (1926-2000), Sohrab Sepehri (1928-1980), Nima Yooshij (1897-1959), and Javad Azar (….-2010).

The majority of the original photographs in this book are spiritual places in Kathmandu, Nepal, and Kamakura, Japan. Mystical concepts in Rumi's poetry, composed in Farsi with thirteenth century syntax, imagery, and symbols, are universal mystical concepts. Photographs in this book also depict universal mystical concepts, but with local imagery and symbols and through different media.

Shahin Motallebi
Los Angeles, California
October 1, 2012

POEM 1

You, the infinite grace, the sudden rapture

ای رستخیز ناگهان وی رحمت بی‌منتها   ای آتشی افروخته در بیشهٔ اندیشه‌ها

امروز خندان آمدی مفتاح زندان آمدی   بر مستمندان آمدی چون بخشش و فضل خدا

خورشید را حاجب تویی امید را واجب تویی   مطلب تویی طالب تویی هم منتها هم مبتدا

در سینه‌ها برخاسته اندیشه را آراسته   هم خویش حاجت خواسته هم خویشتن کرده روا

ای روح‌بخش بی‌بدل وی لذت علم و عمل   باقی بهانه‌ست و دغل کاین علت آمد وان دوا

این سکر بین هل عقل را وین نقل بین هل نقل را   کز بهر نان و بقل را چندین نشاید ماجرا

خامش که بس مستعجلم رفتم سوی پای علم   کاغذ به نه بشکن قلم ساقی درآمد الصلا

You, the infinite grace, the sudden rapture

You, the spark that set the field of thoughts on fire

You, the messenger of joy, arrived to unlock the prisons

You, like God's mercy and wisdom, for the afflicted persons

You, the veil of the Sun, the object of every aspiration

You, the truth, the seeker, the start and the expiration

You, filling our hearts, shaping our thoughts

You, the cause and satisfaction of our wants

You, the peerless creator, joy of our knowledge and action

You, the cure for all ailments, the rest, excuses and illusion

Ignore reason, discourse, and subsistence, be intoxicated

Entered the Tavern of love, my haste and worries all disappeared.

Rumi died suddenly of an unknown illness. His son, Sultan Valad, was at his bed constantly during his last days. Rumi asked Sutan Valad to leave his side and rest for a while. Rumi then started composing his last poem (Poem 14). Sultan Valad took down his father's words while sobbing.

Muslim, Christian, and Jewish residents of Konya were all in mourning for 40 days after Rumi's death. Sadr Eldin Ghoonavi (c. 1213-1276), who was the most prominent philosopher, scientist, and religious figure in Konya at the time, performed the ritual Islamic prayer at Rumi's funeral.

POEM 2

I am intoxicated, you are intoxicated

من بی خود و تو بی خود ما را که برد خانه؟   من چند تو را گفتم کم خور دو سه پیمانه؟

در شهر یکی کس را هشیار نمی‌بینم   هریک بتر از دیگر شوریده و دیوانه

جانا به خرابات آ تا لذت جان بینی   جان را چه خوشی باشد بی صحبت جانانه؟

هر گوشه یکی مستی دستی ز بر دستی   وان ساقی هر هستی با ساغر شاهانه

توقف خراباتی دخلت می و خرجت می   زین وقف به هشیاران مسپار یکی دانه

ای لولی بربط زن تو مست تری یا من   ای پیش چو تو مستی افسون من افسانه

از خانه برون رفتم مستم به پیش آمد   در هر نظرش مضمر صد گلشن و کاشانه

چون کشتی بی لنگر کژ می‌شد و مژ می‌شد   وز حسرت او مرده صد عاقل و فرزانه

گفتم "ز کجایی تو؟" تسخر زد و گفت: "ای جان   نیمم ز ترکستان نیمم ز فرغانه

نیمم ز آب و گل نیمم ز جان و دل   نیمم لب دریا نیمی همه دردانه

گفتم که "رفیقی کن با من که منم خویشت"   گفتا که "بنشناسم من خویش ز بیگانه

من بی دل و دستارم در خانه خمارم   یک سینه سخن دارم هین شرح دهم یا نه؟

در حلقه لگانی می‌باید لنگیدن   این پند نوشیدی از خواجه علیانه

سرمست چنان خوبی کی کم بود از خوبی؟   برخاست فغان آخر از استن حنانه

شمس الحق تبریزی از خلق چه پرهیزی؟   اکنون که در افکندی صد قله فتانه

I am intoxicated, you are intoxicated, who's taking us home?

How many times did I tell you not so much to consume?

I can't find anyone sober in this town

One worse than the other, raptured and ecstatic

Dear Ones, come to the Tavern, enjoy the Divine

What is the point of life without the talk of love?

In every corner, one intoxicated more than the other

By the exalted creation, by the Divine creator

You are a devotee of the Tavern, wine is your business

Don't waste a drop of it on the sobers

Hey you, the lute playing gypsy, who is more intoxicated, me or you

My spell does not bind you, it just amuses you

As I left the house, an intoxicated man approached me

Hidden in his eyes, the secrets of the Divine

Like an anchorless boat, he swayed from side to side

Many wise and brilliant men envious of his stature

I asked him: "where do you come from?" He smiled and said:

Half of me from Turkestan, half from Forghan

Half of me water and mud, half heart and soul

Half of me shells on the shoreline, half a string of pearls

I told him: "befriend me, I am your kin"

He said: "I do not differentiate strangers from kin"

I have abandoned my life for the Tavern

I have a lot to say, can I begin?

In the company of limpers, you must limp

You did not heed the advice of the Wise

Your ecstasy, your rapture has no boundary

Why do you deny us the pleasure of your company?

Shams Tabrizi, why do you avoid us?

Now that you have excited us with so many temptations.

POEM 3

Divine light, the source of our existence

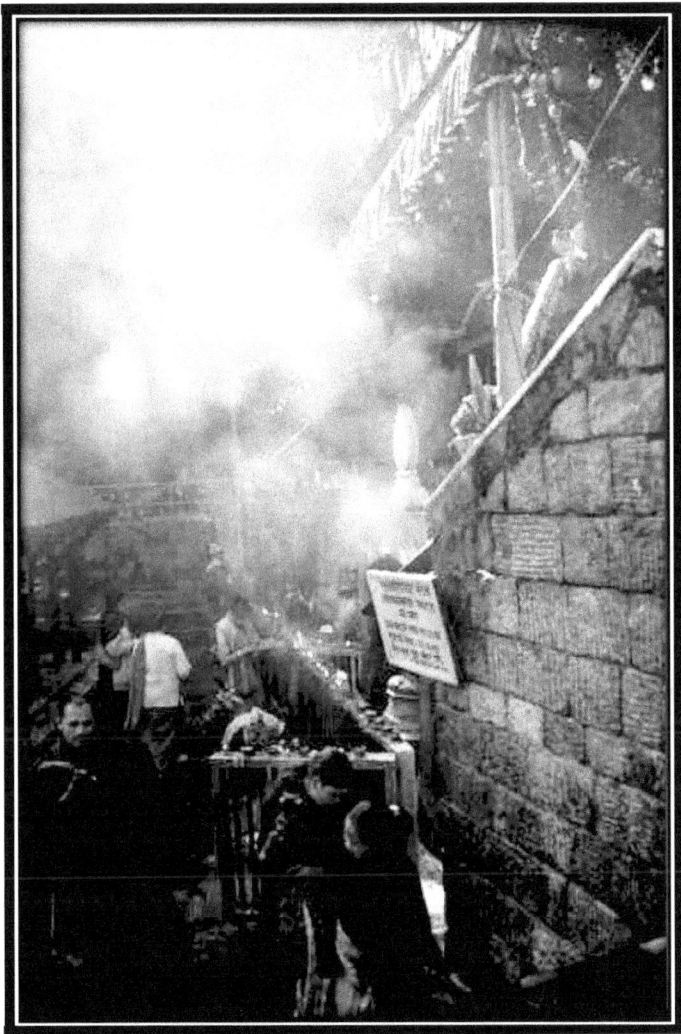

ما زنده به نور کبریاییم   یگانه و سخت آشناییم

مه توبه کند ز خویش بینی   گر ما رخ خود به مه نماییم

در سوزد پر و بال خورشید   چون ما پر و بال بر گشاییم

این هیکل آدم است رو پوش   ما قبله جمله سجده هاییم

آن دم بنگر مبین تو آدم   تا جانت به لطف در رباییم

ابلیس نظر جدا جدا داشت   پنداشت که ما ز حق جداییم

شمس تبریز خود بهانه ست   ماییم به حسن لطف ماییم

با خلق بگو ـ برای روپوش ـ   که "او شاه کریم و ما گداییم"

ما را چه ز شاهی و گدایی   شادیم که شاه را سزاییم

محویم به حسن شمس تبریز   در محو نه او بود نه ماییم

Divine light, the source of our existence

Extremely similar, despite the difference

Beauty of the Moon, brilliance of the Sun

Things bygone, if we showed our true essence

Human body, just an external cover

We are the object and direction of each prayer

Look at the Divine substance, not the body

Let us bless you with our divinity

Satan had a different view of the human design

Thought that we were void of the Divine

Shams Tabriz, just an excuse

We are all blessed with the Divine

With the masses, to keep the cover

Make him the king, you be the beggar

Being the king or the beggar, who cares

We are happy to be worthy of the king, that matters

Divinity in Shams Tabriz overwhelms us

If we looked within, there is no him and there is no us.

Notes Page

POEM 4

You are like my soul, with me, yet hidden

ای با من و پنهان چو دل از دل سلامت می‌کنم   تو کعبه‌ای هر جا روم قصد مقامت می‌کنم

هر جا که هستی حاضری از دور در ما ناظری   شب خانه روشن می‌شود چون یاد نامت می‌کنم

که همچو باز آشنا بر دست تو پر می‌زنم   که چون کبوتر پر زنان آهنگ بامت می‌کنم

گر غایبی مردم چرا آسیب بر دل می‌زنی؟   ور حاضری پس من چرا در سینه دامت می‌کنم؟

دوری به تن لیک از دلم اندر دل تو روزنیست   زان روزن دزدیده من چون مه پیامت می‌کنم

من آینه‌ی دل را ز تو اینجا صقالی می‌دهم   من گوش خود را دفتر لطف کلامت می‌کنم

در گوش تو در هوش تو و اندر دم پرجوش تو   این‌ها چه باشد؟ تو منی وین وصف حامت می‌کنم

ای دل نه اندر ماجرا می‌گفت آن دلبر تو را: هر چند از تو کم شود از خود تمامت می‌کنم

که راست ماند الف که کژ چو حرف مختلف   یک لحظه پخته می‌شوی یک لحظه خامت می‌کنم

گر سالها ره می روی چون مهره‌ای در دست من   چیزی که رامش می‌کنی زان چیز رامت می‌کنم

ای شه حسام الدین حسن می‌گوی با جانان که "من   جان را خلاف معرفت بهر حسامت می‌کنم"

You are like my soul, with me, yet hidden, from the bottom of my heart I greet you

You are like Ka'abe; wherever I am, my heart turns to you

Wherever you are, you are with me; from afar, you keep an eye on me

When I utter your name, my abode lights up

Sometimes like a hawk, I fly away from your arm

Sometimes like a dove, I fly back to your roof top

If you are absent, why the connection to my soul?

If you are present, why do I trap you in my bosom?

You are away from my body, but my soul has a
small window to your soul

From that hidden window I contact you from afar

Purity of your soul purifies me

Divinity of your words elevates me

What's in your words, your mind, your excited soul?

You are me, I generalize your attributes

In the gathering of the Sufis were you not told?

Your attributes are fluid, dependent on my mold

Exalted Hesam Eldin Hassan, tell the Dear Ones

I am your devotee, my soul is yours

POEM 5

Fellow lovers, it's time to leave this world

ای عاشقان ای عاشقان هنگام کوچ است از جهان در گوش جانم می‌رسد طبل رحیل از آسمان

این بانگ‌ها از پیش و پس بانگ رحیل است و جرس هر لحظه‌ای نفس و نفس سر می‌کشد در لامکان

زین شمع‌های سرنگون زین پرده‌های نیلگون خلقی عجب آید برون تا غیب‌ها گردد عیان

زین چرخ دولابی تو را آمد گران خوابی تو را فریاد از این عمر سبک! زنهار از این خواب گران!

ای دل سوی دلدار شو ای یار سوی یار شو ای پاسبان بیدار شو خفته نشاید پاسبان

هر سوی شمع و مشعله هر سوی بانگ و مشغله کامشب جهان حامله زاید جهان جاودان

تو گل بدی و دل شدی جاهل بدی عاقل شدی آن کو کشیدت این چنین آن سو کشاندت کش کشان

اندر کشاکش های او نوش است ناخوش های او   آب است آتش های او بروی مکن رو راگران

در جان نشستن کار او توبه شکستن کار او   از حیله بسیار او این ذره ها لرزان دلان

در من کسی دیگر بود کاین خشم ها از وی جهد   گر آب سوزانی کند ز آتش بود این را بدان

در کف ندارم سنگ من با کس ندارم جنگ من   با کس نگیرم تنگ من زیرا خوشم چون گلستان

پس خشم من زان سر بود وز عالم دیگر بود   این سو جهان آن سو جهان بنشسته من بر آستان

بر آستان آن کس بود کاو ناطق اخرس بود   این رمز گفتی بس بود دیگر مگو در کش زبان

Fellow lovers, it's time to leave this world

Heavens are calling me to depart this world

These calls for departure, we are told

Mark the passage of souls into the void

From the inverted candles in the sky's blue fabric

Comes forth an exalted creation, the mysteries to
unfold

The material world is nothing but a dream

Why this short life? Why this deep sleep?

Dear Ones, find a soul mate; dear friends, find a
mate

Don't fall asleep, you must stay alert

Every corner is teeming with lights and sounds

This is the night of the birth of the everlasting world

You were base, exalted you became; you were ignorant, cognizant you became

Whatever led you this far, would lead you all the way

Embrace the troubles you face in this path

What feels like fire is actually water, be tolerant

The Divine is present in our souls, cause of our transgressions

Extremely resourceful, cause of each particle's vibrations

This anger in me, not from me, is other worldly

Water that burns has fire in it, listen to me

I am not armed; there is no hostility in me

I hold no grudge; I am serene like a flower garden

I am sitting on the threshold of both worlds

The source of my anger is the other world

On the threshold sits only the mute

Enough is said, be discreet, be mute

Shams Tabrizi is an enigmatic figure. However, it is clear from the few historic accounts about Shams, gathered by Rumi followers during Shams' short stay in Konya, that he had an acerbic personality and was a true non-conformist and an iconoclast. Shams did not believe in the formalities and rituals of the Khaneghah system.

Shams' primary criterion for evaluating people was their degree of "love," not scientific knowledge or religiosity. It is not clear if Shams ever composed any poetry, but his love and knowledge of poetry is undisputed. His favorite poets were Sanai (c. 1080-1131), Khaghani (c. 1120-1190), Nezami (c. 1141-1209) and Atar (c. 1145-1220). Interestingly, these poets were also Rumi's favorite poets.

POEM 6

Our desert is limitless

کرانی ندارد بیابان ما   قراری ندارد دل و جان ما

جهان در جهان نقش و صورت گرفت   کدام است از این نقش ها آن ما

چو در ره ببینی بریده سری   که غلتان رود سوی میدان ما

از او پرس از او پرس اسرار ما   کز و بشنوی سرّ پنهان ما

چه بودی که یک گوش پیدا شدی   حریف زبان های مرغان ما

چه بودی که یک مرغ پران شدی   بر او طوق سرّ سلیمان ما

چه گویم؟ چه دانم؟ که این داستان   فزون است از حد و امکان ما

چه گونه زنم دم که هر دم به دم   پریشان تر است این پریشان ما

از این داستان بگذر از من مپرس   که در هم شکسته ست دستان ما

Our desert is limitless

Our heart and soul is restless

Forms are worldly constructs

Which worldly form is us

If you passed a severed head in your path

Rolling down the hill towards us

Ask him; ask him about the Divine secrets

He would reveal our hidden secrets

What if a listener could be found

Who could decipher birds' tongues

What if a flying bird could be found

Who had Solomon's secrets around its neck

What can I say? What do I know?

This tale is beyond what I know

How can I keep talking when each moment

My melancholy is worse than the last moment

Never mind the tale, ask me not

My story; coherent, it is not.

According to the Oxford dictionary of Islam, khaneghah, khanegah, or Khanaqah is the Farsi term for Sufi meetinghouse. Al-Maqrizi (d. 1461) wrote that khanaqahs first appeared in the tenth century and that these buildings were "exclusively dedicated to the worship of God almighty," although other reports refer to their existence as early as the ninth century.

Some of the earliest recorded khanaqahs in Iran were established by Muhammad ibn Karram (d. 839), the founder of the Karrami sect, for his followers. Abu Said ibn Abil-Khayr (d. 1049) was the first to codify and record rules for Sufi novices in the khanaqah. Early classical Iranian Sufi sources employ five different terms— khanaqah, ribat, sumaa, tekke, and zawiyah—practically interchangeably to denote the meetinghouse of the first Sufi fraternities.

POEM 7

To be lost in being lost, that is my religion

کم شدن در کم شدن دین من است   نیستی در هست آیین من است

تا پیاده می‌روم در کوی دوست   سبز خنگ چرخ در زین من است

چون به یک دم صد جهان واپس کنم   بنگرم کام نخستین من است

من چرا کردم جهان گردم چو دوست   در میان جان شیرین من است

شمس تبریزی که فخر اولیاست   "سین" دندان‌هاش "یاسین" من است

To be lost in being lost, that is my religion

To be non-existent in existence, that is my religion

I tread lightly in my Beloved's presence

Key to the secrets of the universe is in my presence

When I finally regress to the moment of creation

I will observe, the first step of my initiation

Why should I wander around the world?

When the Beloved is in my sweet soul

Shams Tabrizi, pride and joy of all creation

The letter "S" in his name, enough for my salvation

POEM 8

Pilgrims of the house of God

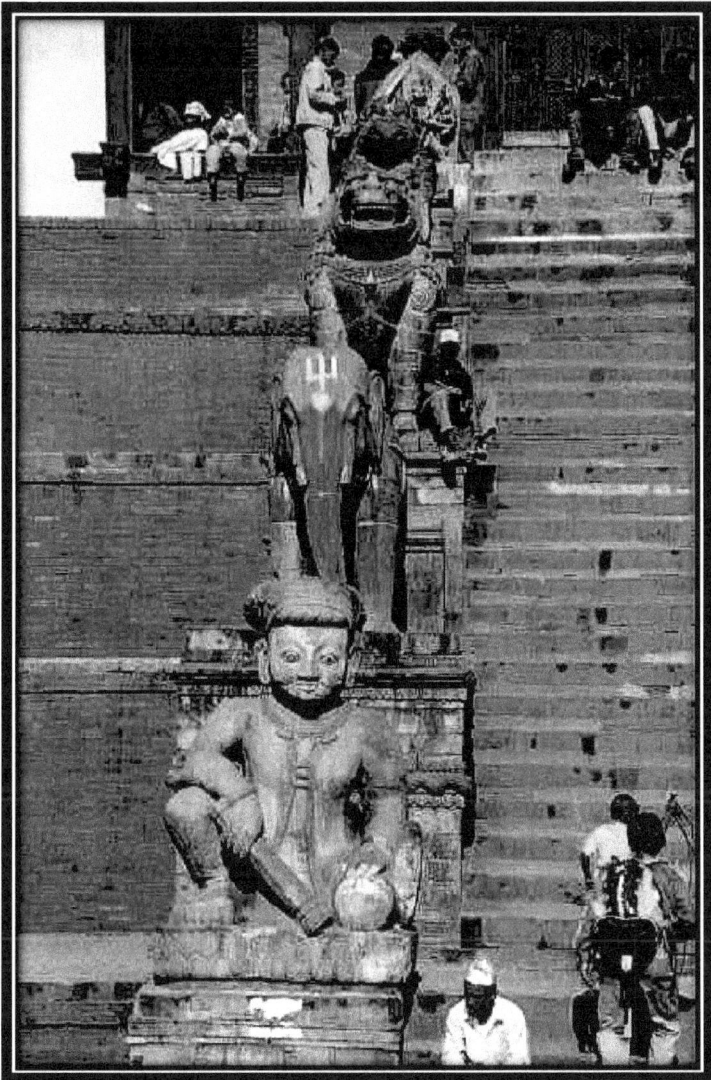

ای قوم به حج رفته کجایید؟ کجایید؟   معشوق همین جاست بیایید بیایید

معشوق تو همسایه دیوار به دیوار   در بادیه سرگشته شما در چه هوایید؟

گر صورت بی صورت معشوق ببینید   هم خواجه و هم خانه و هم کعبه شمایید

ده بار از آن راه بدان خانه برفتید   یک بار از این خانه بر این بام برآیید

آن خانه لطیف است نشان هاش بگفتید   از خواجه آن خانه نشانی بنمایید

یک دسته گل کو اگر آن باغ بدیدت؟   یک گوهر جان کو اگر از بحر خدایید؟

با این همه آن رنج شما گنج شما باد   افسوس که بر رنج شما پرده شمایید

Pilgrims of the house of God, wherever you are

Come back, come back, the Beloved is not so far

The Beloved, closer than your neighbor next door

You are wandering in the Desert, what for?

If the faceless face of the Beloved you seek

Look within, you are what you seek

You have taken the outward path many times

Take the inward path this one time

Knowing the address to the house, a comforting thought

But when you arrived, it was empty, was it not?

If you found the garden where is the flower?

If you found the house, where is the owner?

Your search for the external god, fulfilling, but to no avail

To reach the Beloved, look within, you are the veil

Molavieh is the title given to those Sufis who are members of the original Khaneghah in Konya attended by Rumi and his family members and followers. Rumi appointed Salah Eldin Zarkoob as his successor at the Khaneghah, and after Salah Eldin's death, he appointed Hesam Eldin Chalabi.

After Rumi's death, Hesam Eldin replaced Rumi at the Khaneghah, and after his death, Sultan Valad, Rumi's son, became the head of the Molavieh Khaneghah. Molavieh Khaneghah in present day Konya is still run by descendants of Rumi and the original members.

POEM 9

You nature is different than mine

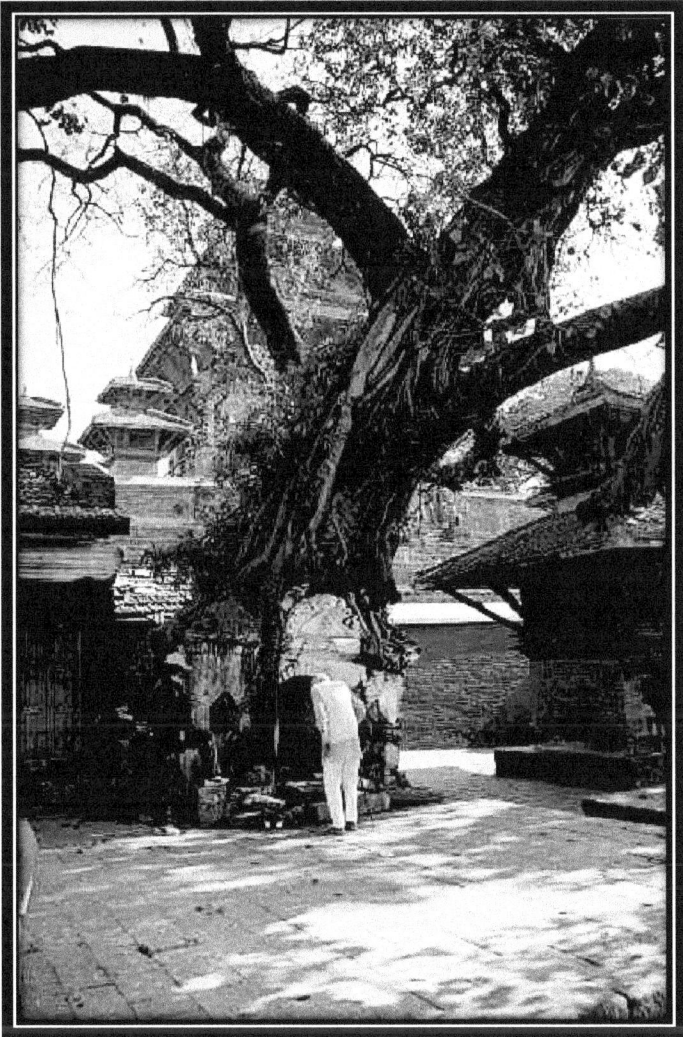

تو نه چنانی که منم من نه چنانم که تویی   تو نه بر آنی که منم من نه بر آنم که تویی

من همه در حکم توام تو همه در خون منی   گر مه و خورشید شوم من کم از آنم که تویی

با همه ای رشک پری چون سوی من برگذری   باش چنین تیزمران تا که بدانم که تویی

دوش گذشتی ز درم بوی نبردم ز تو من   کرد خبر گوش مرا جان و روانم که تویی

چون همه جان رو دیده و دل همچو کیا خاک درت   جان و دلی راچه محل؟ ای دل و جانم که تویی

چون تو مرا کوش کشان بردی از آنجا که منم   بر سر آن مطره‌ها هم بنشانم که تویی

مستم و تو مست زمن سهو خطا جست زمن   من نزیم لیک بدان هم تو رسانم که تویی

زین همه خاموش کنم صبر و صبر نوش کنم   عذر گناهی که کنون گفت زبانم که تویی

Your nature is different than mine

My substance is different than yours

I am at your command, you are in my blood

If I became the Sun and the Moon, I am still beneath you

You, the envy of angels, if you passed me by

Slow down, stay a moment, let me realize you are nearby

Last night you passed by my door, I did not know

But the divinity in me sensed you are close by

Spirituality grows like a plant at your door step

Who cares about spiritual growth? You are my heart and soul

You dragged me out of my comfort zone

Take me to the same level that you are

My intoxication intoxicates you; I am guilt free

You are already enlightened, I will never be

For now, I will keep the secret, I will suffer in silence

For the transgression of uttering your name.

Sufism is the mystical aspect of Islam. Sufis believe in the unity of the creation and the creator, and seek to find the divine reality and the divine truth through love and direct experience of God.

Two primary Sufi practices are Sama, a combination of prayer, singing, and physical movement, and Zekr, recitation of religious text.

POEM 10

My lover is one who

مرا عاشق چنان باید که هر باری که بر خیزد / قیامت‌های پرآتش ز هر سویی برانگیزد

دلی خواهیم چون دوزخ که دوزخ را فرو سوزد / دو صد دریا بشوراند ز موج بحر نگریزد

فلک‌ها را چو مندیلی به دست خویش در پیچد / چراغ لایزالی را چو قندیلی درآویزد

چو شیری سوی جنگ آید دل او چون نهنگ آید / به جز خود پیچ نگذارد و با خود نیز بستیزد

چو هفتصد پرده دل را به نور خود بدراند / ز عرشش این ندا آید: «بنامیزد بنامیزد»

چو از هفتمین دریا به کوه قاف رو آرد / از آن دریا چه گوهرها کنار خاک در ریزد

My lover is one who:

Each time he rises, fiery apocalypses erupt from every corner

Has an infernal spirit that consumes all infernos

Causes hurricanes in two hundred seas, and weathers the storms

Folds the entire universe like a napkin

Hangs up the infinite light like a lantern

Charges into battle like a lion with a whale-size courage

Destroys everything in his path, and then fights
his own ego

Penetrates seven hundred veils and reaches the
Divine with his light

Sounds of adulation for him echo from the Heavens

Crosses the seventh sea on the way to the tallest
mountain; and

Leaves countless treasures in his path.

Konya was part of the vast Islamic world at the time. It was a cosmopolitan city wherein Church and Mosque and Knesset were built next to each other and adherents of different faiths lived in Konya in harmony. The early permanent settlements in and around Konya date back to the Neolithic, Paleolithic and Bronze ages.

Present day Konya is in the Central Anatolia Region of Turkey. It is the seventh most populous city in Turkey.

POEM 11

Praise love, praise my love, dear God

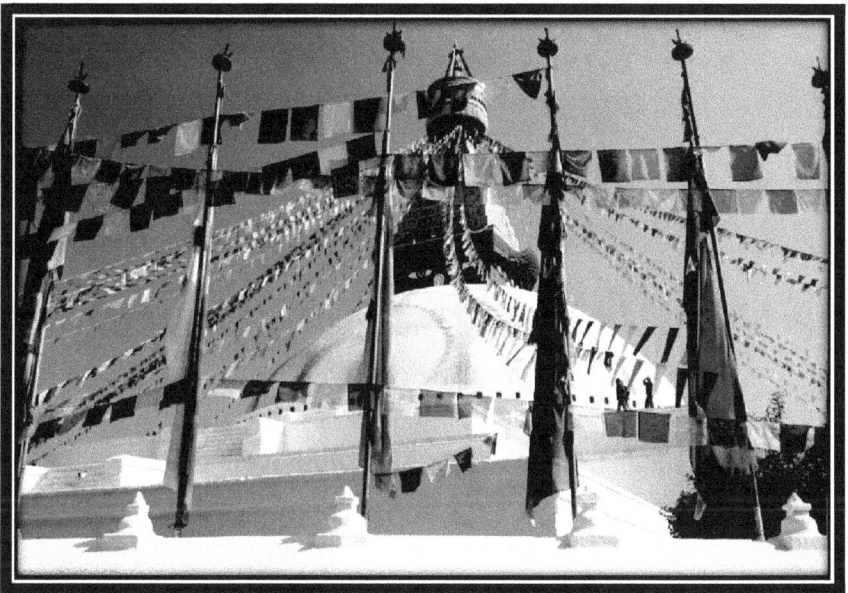

زهی عشق زهی که ماراست خدایا   چه نغز است و چه خوب است و چه زیباست! خدایا

چه کریم چه کریم! از این عشق چو خورشید   چه پنهان و چه پنهان و چه پیداست خدایا

زهی ماه زهی ماه زهی باده همراه   که جان را و جهان را بیاراست خدایا

زهی شور زهی شور! که انگیخته عالم   زهی کار زهی بار که آن جاست! خدایا

فروریخت فروریخت شهنشاه سواران   زهی گرد زهی گرد که برخاست! خدایا

فتادیم فتادیم بدان‌سان که نخیزیم   ندانیم ندانیم چه غوغاست خدایا

زهرکوی زهرکوی یکی دود دگرگون   دگربار دگربار چه سوداست خدایا

نه دامی‌ست نه زنجیر همه بستهٔ چراییم؟   چه بندست! چه زنجیر! چه برپاست خدایا

چه نقشی‌ست! چه نقشیت! در این تابه دل‌ها   غریب است غریب است زبالاست خدایا

خموشید خموشید که تا فاش نگردید   که اغیار گرفته‌ست چپ و راست خدایا

Praise love, praise my love, dear God

So elegant, so fine, so beautiful, dear God

Warmth of this love, like the warmth of the Sun

Try to keep it hidden, but it shines through, dear God

Praise the Moon, praise the Moon and the wine

That adorns the Beloved and the world, dear God

Praise the passion, praise the passion that incited creation

Praise the effort, praise the outcome, dear God

The Beloved has collapsed, has collapsed

Praise the dust, praise the dust that arose, dear God

We have fallen down, fallen so as not to rise again

Why the clamor, the clamor, dear God

Smoke is coming out of every corner, every corner

Why the madness, the madness again, dear God

There is no trap, no chain, why are we in fetters?

What rope, what chain is clamping our feet, dear God?

What design, what design in our hearts?

It's different, it's different, it's transcendent, dear God

I should be silent, I should be discreet

Strangers are all around me, dear God.

POEM 12

My heart's desire, come reveal yourself

ای هوس‌های دلم باری بیا رویی نما   ای مراد و حاصلم باری بیا رویی نما

مشکل و شوریده‌ام چون زلف تو چون زلف تو   ای کشاده مشکلم باری بیا رویی نما

از ره و منزل مکو دیگر مکو دیگر مکو   ای تو راه و منزلم باری بیا رویی نما

تا ز نیکی و ز بدی من واقفم من واقفم   از جمالت غافلم باری بیا رویی نما

تا نسوزد عقل من در عشق تو در عشق تو   غافلم نی عاقلم باری بیا رویی نما

شه صلاح‌الدین که تو هم حاضری هم غایبی   ای عجوبه واصلم باری بیا رویی نما

My heart's desire, come reveal yourself

My wish, my end, come reveal yourself

I am entangled and frenzied, like your hair

Untangle my problems, come reveal yourself

Don't talk about paths and destinations

My path and my destination, come reveal yourself

I am aware of good, I am aware of evil

I miss your presence, come reveal yourself

Until your love consumes my reason

I am ignorant, I am unwise, come reveal yourself

Exalted Salah Eldin, you are present, yet absent

You have achieved enlightenment, come reveal yourself.

Rumi's magnum opus is Masnavi Maanavi. It is widely believed that Hesam Eldin Chalabi asked Rumi to write a masnavi (style of poetry) in the meter of Atar's Mantegh al Teir and in the style of Sanai's Elahi Nameh. Rumi reached into his turban and handed to Hesam Eldin the first 18 lines that he had already composed (Poem 15).

The best English translation of Masnavi is by Reynold A. Nicholson.

Rumi With A View
To Other
Persian Mystic Poets

Shahin Mowlalifar

POEM 13

I was dead, alive I became

مرده بدم زنده شدم گریه بدم خنده شدم   دولت عشق آمد و من دولت پاینده شدم

دیده سیر است مرا جان دلیر است مرا   زهره شیر است مرا زهره تابنده شدم

گفت که "دیوانه نی لایق این خانه نی"   رفتم دیوانه شدم سلسله بندنده شدم

گفت که "سرمست نی رو که از این دست نی" رفتم و سرمست شدم وز طرب آکنده شدم

گفت که "تو کشته نی در طرب آغشته نی"   پیش رخ زنده کنش کشته و افکنده شدم

گفت که "تو زیرکی مست خیالی و شکی"   گول شدم هول شدم وز همه برکنده شدم

گفت که "تو شمع شدی قبله این جمع شدی"   جمع نیم شمع نیم دود پراکنده شدم

گفت که "بیئنی و سری پیشرو و راهبری"   شیخ نیم پیش نیم امر تورا بنده شدم

گفت که "با بال و پری من پر و بالت ندهم"   در هوس بال و پرش بی پر و پرکنده شدم

گفت مرا دولت نو: "راه مرو رنجه مشو   زان که من از لطف و کرم سوی تو آینده شدم"

گفت مرا عشق کهن: "از بر ما نقل مکن"   گفتم : "آری نکنم ساکن و باشنده شدم"

چشمه خورشید تویی سایه که بید منم   چون که زدی بر سر من پست و گدازنده شدم

تابش جان یافت دلم واشد و بشکافت دلم   اطلس نو بافت دلم دشمن این ژنده شدم

صورت جان وقت سحر لاف همی زد ز بطر   بنده و خربنده بدم شاه و خداونده شدم

شکر کند کاغذ تو از شکر بی حد تو   کامد او در بر من با وی ماننده شدم

شکر کند خاک دژم از فلک و چرخ بخم   کز نظر و گردش او نور پذیرنده شدم

شکر کند چرخ فلک از ملک و ملک و ملک   کز کرم و بخشش او روشن و بخشنده شدم

شکر کند عارف حق کز همه بردیم سبق   بر زبر هفت طبق اختر رخشنده شدم

از توام ای شهره قمر در من و در خود بنگر   کز اثر خنده تو گلشن خنده شدم

باش چو شطرنج روان خامش و خود جمله زبان   کز رخ آن شاه جهان فرخ و فرخنده شدم

I was dead, alive I became; I was in tears, laughter I became

Power of love arrived, eternal I became

I am contented, I am courageous

I am lion-hearted, shining Venus I became

Raptured and worthy of this Tavern you are not, he said

I left, raptured and insane I became

Leave here, you are not intoxicated by love, he said

I left, intoxicated and full of joy I became

Your ego is still alive, you are not ecstatic, he said

In front of his life-giving self, annihilated I became

You are clever, you are full of doubts, he said

Startled and insecure, a recluse I became

You are a beacon, the center of attention, he said

Center I am not, beacon I am not, scattered smoke I became

You are the Sheikh, you are the leader, he said

Sheikh I am not, leader I am not, your servant I became

You are conceited, I will not praise you, he said

Yearning for his approval, down to earth I became

Do not leave, take no offense, he said

Kindness and generosity has brought me to you

Let go of the story of ancient love, he said

I acquiesced, firm and steady I became

You are Sun's stream, I am just a shadow

Since you shone on me, humble and melted I
became

Power of love entered my heart, open and wide it became

I let go of the old one, brand new it became

My true self, at dawn, boasted about ecstasy

Slave and a servant I was, a divine king I became

The whole creation is grateful of his presence

Because of his mercy and grace, forgiving and enlightened I became

Thanks to the Divine grace, I surpassed everyone

Above the sky's seventh layer, a shining star I became

I am with you; take a look at me and at yourself

With a hint of your smile, a happy soul I became

Like a chess player, I should be silent, yet mindful

In the castle of the king of the world, joyful and auspicious I became

POEM 14

Go rest a while, let me be alone

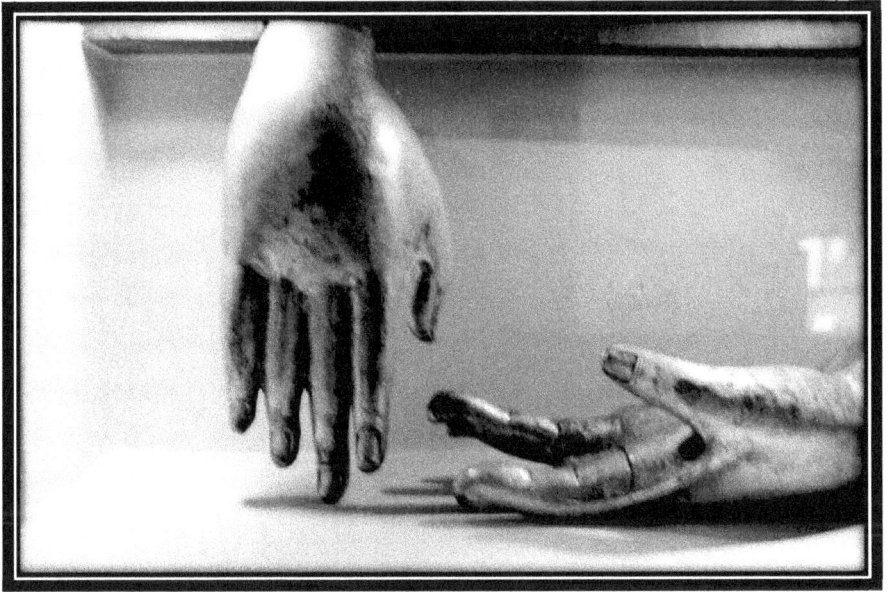

رو سر بنه به بالین تنها مرا رها کن | ترک من خراب شبگرد مبتلا کن

مائیم و موج سودا شب تا به روز تنها | خواهی بیا ببخشا خواهی برو جفا کن

از من گریز! تا تو هم در بلا نیفتی | بگزین ره سلامت ترک ره بلا کن

مائیم و آب دیده در کنج غم خزیده | بر آب دیده ما صد جای آسیا کن

خیره کشی‌ست مارا دارد دلی چو خارا | بکشد کش نگوید: تدبیر خونبها کن

ای زرد روی عاشق تو صبر کن وفا کن   بر شاه خوبرویان واجب وفا نباشد

پس من چه گونه گویم کاین درد را دوا کن؟   دردی ست غیر مردن آن را دوا نباشد

با دست اشارتم کرد که عزم سوی ما کن   در خواب دوش پیری در کوی عشق دیدم

از برق این زمرد هین دفع اژدها کن   گر اژدهاست بر ره عشق است چون زمرد

تاریخ بو علی گو تنبیه بوالعلا کن   بس کن که بی خودم من ور تو هنر فزایی

Go rest a while, let me be alone

Leave me, the intoxicated, the wanderer, the lovelorn

It's me, my loneliness, and my melancholic mind

Come back and forgive, or go and be unkind

Run away from me, choose the safe path

Escape trouble, leave the treacherous path

I am all tears, so much sadness I feel

Volume of my tears could turn a water-wheel

My Beloved, with a heart of stone

If he killed someone, needs not to atone

Loyalty is not for the most beautiful

You, the lovelorn, be patient, be faithful

Death alone can cure my pain

Asking you for a cure would be in vain

In my dream last night a mystic appeared

In the Tavern of love we were when he said:

"If the dragon in the path to the Beloved you fear

Brilliance of love will make all obstacles disappear"

I am beside myself, void of any desire

To lecture on history, religion, or another.

POEM 15

Listen to the reed's narration

بشنو از نی چون حکایت می‌کند	از جدایی‌ها شکایت می‌کند

کز نیستان تا مرا ببریده اند	از نفیرم مرد و زن نالیده اند

سینه خواهم شرحه شرحه از فراق	تا بگویم شرح درد اشتیاق

هر کسی کو دور ماند از اصل خویش	باز جوید روزگار وصل خویش

من به هر جمعیتی نالان شدم	جفت بد حالان و خوش حالان شدم

هر کسی از ظن خود شد یار من	از درون من نجست اسرار من

سر من از نالهٔ من دور نیست   لیک چشم و گوش را آن نور نیست

تن ز جان و جان ز تن مستور نیست   لیک کس را دید جان دستور نیست

آتشست این بانگ نای و نیست باد   هر که این آتش ندارد نیست باد

آتش عشقست کاندر نی فتاد   جوشش عشقست کاندر می فتاد

نی حریف هر که از یاری برید   پرده‌هایش پرده‌های ما درید

همچو نی زهری و تریاقی که دید   همچو نی دمساز و مشتاقی که دید

نی حدیث راه پر خون می‌کند   قصه‌های عشق مجنون می‌کند

محرم این هوش جز بیهوش نیست   مرزبان را مشتری جز گوش نیست

Listen to the reed's narration

Complaining about its separation

Since I was cut off from the reed-bed

To my music, men and women have wailed

If your heart aches of longing

Listen to my story of the pain of yearning

Anyone removed from his original source

Seeks reunion with his source

I have played my music for all

Some of them sad, some jovial

Each had enjoyed my sound by himself

None had sought to uncover my true self

My music drapes my secrets, a thin cover

Which eyes and ears fail to uncover

Body and soul are discoverable to each other

But discovering the soul is not preordained

Reed's music is made up of fire, not air

Those who lack the fire, do expire

It is the fire of love that the reed emanates

It is the power of love that the wine ferments

Reed is companion to separated lovers

Its high notes penetrates our secrets

Reed is the cure for any poison

Reed is the broken heart's companion

Reed tells stories of pain and suffering

Tales of love unfulfilled

Only the intoxicated appreciates the reed

Lonely's only friend is the sound of the reed.

POEM 16

Hey bartender, pour me some wine

الا یا ایها الساقی ادر کاساً و ناولها   که عشق آسان نمود اول ولی افتاد مشکلها

به بوی نافه‌ای کاخر صبا زان طره بگشاید   ز تاب جعد مشکینش چه خون افتاد در دلها

مرا در منزل جانان چه امن عیش چون هر دم   جرس فریاد می‌دارد که بربندید محملها

به می سجاده رنگین کن گرت پیر مغان گوید   که سالک بی خبر نبود ز راه و رسم منزلها

شب تاریک و بیم موج و گردابی چنین هایل   کجا دانند حال ما سبکباران ساحلها

همه کارم ز خودکامی به بدنامی کشید آخر   نهان کی ماند آن رازی کزو سازند محفلها

حضوری گر همی خواهی ازو غایب مشو حافظ   متی ما تلق من تهوی دع الدنیا و اهملها

Hey bartender, pour me some wine

It seemed easy at first, but love and trouble entwine

Morning breeze uncurls my beloved's perfumed hair

Many hearts ache with desire for her

How can I enjoy her company for a moment?

When I have to depart any given moment

Listen to the Wise and drink wine

The path to the Beloved is through wine

Standing firm on the shore, the faithful believers

Know not the challenges faced by the seekers

Non-conformity led to my infamy

It's the talk of the town, it defies secrecy

Hafez, if you seek the eternal Beloved

Once achieved, let go of the things desired.

Shams Eldin Mohammad Hafez was born in Shiraz, Iran circa 1315 C.E. and died in Shiraz circa 1390. Divan of Hafez is the most popular classical collection of poems in Iran. Hafez's mystical poetry is loved by all Farsi speaking countries. His poems are an integral part of Iran's classical music.

Hafez's tomb in Shiraz is a popular tourist attraction. Saadi's tomb is also located in Shiraz, not far from Hafez's tomb.

POEM 17

Human beings are all interrelated

بنی آدم اعضای یکدیگرند   که در آفرینش ز یک گوهرند

چو عضوی به درد آورد روزگار   دگر عضوها را نماند قرار

تو کز محنت دیگران بی غمی   نشاید که نامت نهند آدمی

Human beings are all interrelated

From the same substance are all created

If one part suffers

So do all the others

You, who are indifferent to others suffering

Do not deserve to be called a human being

Saadi was born circa 1203 C.E in the city of Shiraz, in the province of Fars, Iran and died in Shiraz circa 1294. Saadi's greatest works are Boostan (Orchard) and Golestan (Flower Garden). His most famous poem, also translated by me in this book, is depicted at the entrance to the Hall of Nations in New York City, with the following English translation:

Of one Essence is the Human Race,
Thusly has Creation put the Base;
One Limb impacted is sufficient,
For all Others to feel the Mace
The Unconcern'd with Others' Plight
Are but Brutes with Human Face

POEM 18

One Moonlit night, without you

بی تو مهتاب شبی باز از آن کوچه گذشتم

همه تن چشم شدم خیره به دنبال تو گشتم

شوق دیدار تو لبریز شد از جام وجودم

شدم آن عاشق دیوانه که بودم

در نهانخانه جانم گل یاد تو درخشید

باغ صد خاطره خندید

عطر صد خاطره پیچید

یادم آمد که شبی با هم از آن کوچه گذشتیم

پر گشودیم و در آن خلوت دلخواسته نشستیم

ساعتی بر لب آن جوی نشستیم

تو همه راز جهان ریخته در چشم سیاهت

من همه محو تماشای نگاهت

آسمان صاف و شب آرام

بخت خندان و زمان رام

خوشه ماه فروردین تختهٔ در آب

شاخه‌ها دست برآورده به مهتاب

شب و صحرا و گل و سنگ

همه دل داده به آواز شباهنگ

یادم آمد تو به من گفتی:

از این عشق حذر کن

لحظه‌ای چند بر این آب نظر کن

آب آیینهٔ عشق گذران است

تو که امروز نگاهت به نگاهی نگران است

باش فردا که دلت با دگران است

تا فراموش کنی چندی از این شهر سفر کن

با تو گفتم: حذر از عشق؟ ندانم

سفر از پیش تو هرگز نتوانم نتوانم

روز اول که دل من به تمنای تو پر زد

چون کبوتر لب بام تو نشستم

تو به من سنگ زدی من نه رمیدم نه گسستم

باز گفتم که:

تو صیادی و من آهوی دشتم

تا به دام تو در افتم همه جا گشتم و گشتم

حذر از عشق ندانم نتوانم

اشکی از شاخه فرو ریخت

مرغ شب ناله تلخی زد و بگریخت

اشک در چشم تو لرزید

ماه بر عشق تو خندید

یادم آمد که:

دگر از تو جوابی نشنیدم

پای در دامن اندوه کشیدم

نه گسستم نه رمیدم

رفت در ظلمت غم آن شب و شبهای دگر هم

نگر فتی دگر از عاشق آزرده خبر هم

نکنی دیگر از آن کوچه گذر هم

بی تو اما

به چه حالی من از آن کوچه گذشتم

One Moonlit night, without you,

I passed that alley again

I became all eyes, looked all over for you

The enthusiasm of seeing you overwhelmed me

I became the same crazy lover that I used to be

In the abyss of my soul the flower of   your memory
glowed

The sound of a hundred laughs

The scent of a hundred perfumes

I remembered the night that we passed that alley

We stretched our wings and roamed around in

that well-desired privacy

We sat by that brook for a while

You, with all the secrets of the world in your black eyes

I, totally fascinated and mesmerized by your look

Sky was clear

Night was calm

Luck was smiling

Time was tame

Moon's cluster had fallen in the water

Twigs had branched out towards the Moonlight

The night and the desert and the flower and the stone

All infatuated by the song of the nightingales

I recalled that you told me:

Avoid this love!

Glance at this water for a moment

Love is like running water

It is transient

You might be obsessed with someone today

But tomorrow, your heart would be with another

To forget, leave this city for a while

I replied:

Avoiding love? Don't know how

Leaving you, can never do, impossible

The first day

When my heart fell for you

Like a dove, I sat on your roof

You hit me with a stone, I persisted

I did not shy away

I said:

You are the hunter and I am the gazelle

To fall into your trap, I searched everywhere

Avoiding love

No way; Impossible

A teardrop fell from the twig

The owl, groaned and fled

Your eyes were tearful

Moon laughed at your love

I remembered that

I never heard from you again

Submerged in my grief

I did not break away

I did not shy away

That night, and the following nights, were gloomy and dark

You never wondered about the tormented lover

You never passed that alley again

Without you, it was so hard to pass that alley again.

Fereydoon Moshiri is probably the most famous contemporary poet in Modern Iran. He was born in Tehran, Iran in 1926. His poetic style was a major influence on other Iranian poets looking for a new way to express their thoughts.

Moshiri's poetry inspires us by exciting our senses and challenging our minds. Moshiri's best poem, in my view, is the Alley, Poem 18 in this book.

POEM 19

I wish for

دلم می خواست سقف معبد هستی فرو میریخت

بهاری جاودان آغوش وامی کرد

جهان در موجی از زیبایی و خوبی شنامی کرد

بهشت عشق می خندید

به روی آسمان آبی آرام

پرستوهای مهر و دوستی پرواز میکردند

به روی بامها ناقوس آزادی صدامی کرد

I wish for:

The ceiling of the temple of existence to collapse,

and

The inviting arms of an eternal Spring

The world to swim in a wave of beauty and goodness, and

The paradise of love to smile at a serene blue sky

The swallows of kindness and friendship to take flight, and

The sound of freedom to echo from the roof tops.

POEM 20

Traveling breeze, tell us

ای نسیم رهگذر به ما بگو

این جوانه‌های باغ زندگی

این شکوفه‌های عشق

از سموم وحشی کدام شوره زار

رفته رفته خار می‌شوند؟

این کبوتران برج دوستی

از غبار جادوی کدام کهکشان

گرگهای هار می‌شوند؟

Traveling breeze, tell us:

Noxious weeds of which salt-land
gradually turn the young leaves of
the garden of life and the blossoms
of love into thorns?

Magical stardust of which galaxy turn
doves of the tower of friendship
into rabid wolves?

POEM 21

Who are you, that without you

تو کیستی که من اینگونه بی تو بی تابم   شب از هجوم خیال تو نمی برد خوابم

تو چیستی که من از موج هر تبسم تو   بسان قایق سرگشته روی گردابم

Who are you, that without you, I am so restless

Dream of you rushes in all night, I am sleepless

What are you, that a hint of your smile

Makes me feel like a raft on a whirlpool.

Moshiri's style of poetry encompasses both the beauty of form and musicality of the classical poetic style, as well as the fluidity and freedom associated with the "new poetry" of the 20th century, initiated by the father of Iran's modern poetry, Nima Yooshij (Poem 24).

POEM 22

Where is the friend's house?

خانه دوست کجاست؟

در افق بود که پرسید سوار

آسمان مکثی کرد

رهگذر شاخه نوری که به لب داشت به تاریکی شن ها بخشید و به

انگشت نشان داد سپیداری و گفت:

نرسیده به درخت

کوچه باغی است که از خواب خدا سبزتر است

و در آن عشق به اندازه پرهای صداقت آبی است

می روی تا ته آن کوچه که از پشت بلوغ سر بدر می آورد

پس به سمت گل تنهایی می پیچی

دو قدم مانده به گل

پای فواره جاوید اساطیر زمان می مانی

و تراتر سی شفاف فرا می گیرد

در صمیمیت سیال فضا خش خشی می شنوی!

کودکی می بینی

رفته از کاج بلندی بالا جوجه بردارد از لانهٔ نور

از او می پرسی

خانهٔ دوست کجاست؟

Where is the friend's house?

Rider was at the horizon when he asked.

The sky paused.

The passerby bestowed the ray of light on his lips to the darkness of the sands and pointed to a white poplar and said:

Before the tree, there is a boulevard greener than God's dream

Where love is as blue as the feathers of honesty

Passed maturity, turn towards the flower of loneliness

Two steps before the flower, in front of
the eternal fountain of myths

While overwhelmed by a transparent fear,

Under the flowing sincerity of space,

You will hear a rustle,

You will see a child,

Climbed on top a tall pine to steal a chick
from the nest of light,

Ask him

Where is the friend's house?

Sohrab Sepehri was born in the city of Kashan, Iran in 1928. Sepehri's favorite subject matters were "nature" and "living in harmony with nature," very similar to the Taoist view.

In Taoism, one who lives in harmony with the natural forces lives a happy and fulfilled life. The selected Sepehri poems in this book are indicative of his naturalist view of life.

In Sepehri's poems one frequently encounters the concept of Tao (path, way, principle, flow of nature) and the concept of Wu-Wei (action through inaction) wherein one harmonizes his actions or intents with the natural flow of the universe.

Sohrab Sepehri died in Tehran in 1980.

POEM 23

Wherever I am, be it

هر کجا هستم باشم

آسمان مال من است

پنجره

فکر

هوا

عشق

زمین مال من است

چه اهمیت دارد

گاه اگر می روید قارچهای غربت

چشمها را باید شست

جور دیگر باید دید

آب تنی کردن در حوضچه اکنون است

زندگی بال و پری دارد

با وسعت مرگ

پرشی دارد به اندازه عشق

زندگی چیزی نیست که لب طاقچه عادت از یاد

من و تو برود

Wherever I am, be it

Sky belongs to me

Window

Thought

Air

Love

Earth is mine

It does not matter if the mushrooms
of nostalgia grow occasionally

Wash your eyes

Look from another angle

Now is the time for bathing in the pool

Life has wings and feathers

As wide as death

And a range as long as love

Life is not something for me
and you to forget

Left unnoticed

On the niche of habit.

POEM 24

Hey you!

آی آدمها که بر ساحل نشسته شاد و خندانید

یک نفر در آب دارد می سپارد جان

یک نفر دارد که دست و پای دائم می زند

روی این دریای تند و تیره و سنگین که می دانید

آن زمان که مست هستید از خیال دست یابیدن به دشمن

آن زمان که پیش خود بیهوده پندارید

که گر قید دست ناتوان را

ناتوانائی بهتر را پدید آرید

آن زمان که تنگ می بندید

بر کمرهاتان کمربند

در چه هنگامی بگویم من؟

یک نفر در آب دارد می‌کند جان قربان!

آی آدم‌ها که بر ساحل بساط دلگشا دارید!

نان به سفره جامه‌تان بر تن

یک نفر در آب می‌خواند شما را

موج سنگین را به دست خسته می‌کوبد

باز می‌دارد دهان با چشم از وحشت دریده

سایه‌هاتان را ز راه دور دیده

آب را بلعیده در گود کبود و هر زمان بی‌تابیش افزون

می‌کند زین آب‌ها بیرون

گاه سر گه پا

آی آدم‌ها!

او از راه دور این کهنه جهان را باز می‌پاید

مینید فریاد و امید کمک دارد

آی آدمها که روی ساحل آرام در کار تماشایید!

موج می کوبد به روی ساحل خاموش

پخش می گردد چنان مستی به جای افتاده بس مدهوش

میرود نعره زنان وین بانک باز از دور می آید:

"آی آدم ها"....

و صدای باد هر دم دلگزارتر

در صدای باد بانک او رهاتر

از میان آب های دور و نزدیک

باز در گوش این نداها:

"آی آدمها....."

Hey you!

Enjoying yourselves on the shore

Someone is drowning in the water

Someone is flouncing constantly

In this heavy, dusky and troubled sea that you all know

At times, when you are high on the dream of victory
over your enemies

At times, when you vainly believe that by helping
a needy person you have participated in
creating a better potential

At times when you have tightened your belts

When shall I say?

Someone's precious life is coming to an end

Hey you!

Having a pleasant picnic at the beach

Bread in your plate, clothes on your body

Someone in the water is calling you

Fatigue is overcoming him as he fights the heavy waves

With an open mouth and dreadful eyes

Has seen your shadows from afar

Has swallowed water in the dark blue abyss

Growing increasingly restless

Barely succeeds in keeping above water

Sometimes his feet, sometimes his head

Hey you!

He is yearning from afar for this old world

Crying loudly, hoping for help

Hey you!

Who are watching, standing on the serene strand

Waves are pounding the silent shore

Spreading wide, like an unconscious drunkard

Surging with a roar, but you can hear this
clamor from afar

Hey you.......

And as the roar of the winds grows louder

His clamor in the hard wind wanes

From the close and distant waters

There is still a murmur

Hey you....

POEM 25

Like a reed, I lament my grieving heart

هر دمی چون نی از دل نالان شکوه ها دارم

روی دل هر شب تا سحرگاهان با خدا دارم

هر نفس آهی است از دل خونین

لحظه های عمر بی سامان می رود سنگین

اشک خون آلود اندامان می کند رنگین

به سکوت سرد زمان به خزان زرد زمان

نه زمان را درد کسی نه کسی را درد زمان

بهار مردمی هم دی شد

زمان مهربانی هم طی شد

آه از این دم سردی ها خدایا

آه از این دم سردی ها خدایا

نه امیدی در دل من که گشاید مشکل من

نه فروغ روی مهی که فروزد محفل من

نه همزبان درد آگاهی که ناله ای خرد با آهی

داد از این بی دردی ها خدایا

داد از این بی دردی ها خدایا

نه صفایی به دم سازی به جان می

که گرد غم ز دل شوید

که بگویم راز پنهان که چه دردی دارم بر جان

وای از این بی همرازی ها خدایا

وای از این بی همرازی ها خدایا

وه که به حسرت عمر گرانی سرشد

همچو شراره از دل آذر بر شد و خاکستر شد

یک نفس زد و هدر شد

یک نفس زد و هدر شد

روزگار من بسر شد.

Like a reed, I lament my grieving heart with each breath

Each night, I pray in silence until Dawn's early light

Every breath is a sigh that emanates from my broken heart

Moments of my unsettled life pass me by solemnly

As the bloodstained tears make my body colorful

The yellow autumns of time passed me by in cold silence

Beware!

Time has no sympathy

The Spring of life is over

The time of kindness is gone

Oh God, I am tired of this unpleasantness

Oh God, I am tired of this unpleasantness

I have no hope for a solution to my problems

Nor do I have a lover whose brightness
could illuminate my abode

Or a sympathetic companion

Who sighs when I open my heart

Oh God, I cannot stand the indifference

Oh God, I cannot stand the indifference

Intoxication brings me no joy

Dusts of sorrow cling to my heart

Sobriety is unbearable

I need to confide in someone

Jealousy

Regret

My life is wasted

Like a spark

It came to an end

My life is over

The harp of my love

Played the song of madness

Pupils of my eyes turned red

Impatience

Fantasy

Self deception

What an unfortunate fantasy

What an unfulfilled hope

Oh God, deliver me from illusion

Oh God, deliver me from self deception

Rumi With A View
To Other
Persian Mystic Poets

Shideh Etaat

www.ingramcontent.com/pod-product-compliance
Lightning Source LLC
Chambersburg PA
CBHW052005090426
42741CB00008B/1557